AND SHIRA IMAGINED

Giora Carmi

THE JEWISH PUBLICATION SOCIETY   PHILADELPHIA | NEW YORK | JERUSALEM   5748 | 1988

For Liane, Ore, and Ilil

Copyright © 1988 by Giora Carmi
First edition   All rights reserved
Printed in China

Library of Congress Cataloging in Publication Data

Karmi, Giyora.
   And Shira imagined.
   Summary: A young girl visits Israel and envisions
the history of the sites she sees.
   1. Israel—Description and travel—Juvenile
literature. [1. Israel—Description and travel]
I. Title.
DS107.4.K335   1988   915.694'0454   87-3648
ISBN 978-0-8276-0899-3

Designed by ADRIANNE ONDERDONK DUDDEN

Shira and her parents had just arrived in Israel.

"This is like no other country," Shira's father said.

"It's an ancient holy land for many religions.

It's the land of the Bible. And it's a modern

country, too, with tall buildings and factories."

In Tel Aviv Shira's mother said, "Look around. This is a busy modern city. But eighty years ago there was nothing here, just white hills of sand. Imagine, this city appeared like a miracle out of the sand."

And Shira imagined.

In Caesarea Shira saw old stone columns and roads and a large, 2000-year-old stadium. Shira was standing near curved stone arches when her father said, "Imagine, this was once a great port city. In the water, right here, were boats loaded with spices, silks and other things."

And Shira imagined.

Shira and her parents visited a kibbutz. Shira's mother said, "The people who live here are like one big family. Some people cook for everyone. A few milk all the cows. And some pick the fruit. And everyone here shares what he or she has with everyone else. Can you imagine that, Shira, sharing everything you have with so many people?"

And Shira imagined.

Shira and her family rode a tramway to the top of a steep cliff. Shira got off and looked at the remains of an old fortress. "This is Massada," Shira's father said. "Almost 2000 years ago there were buildings here, and storehouses with food and water. During a war with the mighty Romans, hundreds of Jews lived here. The Roman Army tried to get up here, but for three years the Jews held them off. Can you imagine that, Shira, living here while below Roman soldiers are trying to fight their way up?"

And Shira imagined.

Shira and her parents traveled to Eilat. They stood on the beach, surrounded by sand, mountains, and water. "This is the Red Sea," Shira's mother said. Soon we'll be swimming in it; under the water we'll breathe through these snorkels and look around. Just imagine, we'll be looking at thousands of fish and swimming with them."

And Shira imagined.

In Jerusalem Shira and her parents visited the Israel Museum, the Biblical Zoo, and the Knesset building, where Israel's government meets. They saw the Western Wall, the last remaining wall of the Holy Temple. Then they saw King David's Tower. Shira's mother said, "At one time King David walked here. Can you imagine that, Shira? Maybe he even sat right here and played his harp."

And Shira imagined.

After two weeks in Israel, Shira's father said, "We'll visit again. I hope one day we can come to live in Israel. It's our homeland, you know."
And Shira's mother said, "But now we're on our way home. Just imagine, Shira, soon you'll be in your own room."

And Shira imagined being home again in her room with all her toys.

ravel in my imagination.

ing I imagine comes from something

r known in the real world. So I take

give thanks to good old reality,

my imagination.